easy
italian

easy
italian

This edition first published in the UK in 2000 by Hamlyn for WHSmith, Greenbridge Road, Swindon SN3 3LD

Copyright © 2000 Octopus Publishing Group Limited

Octopus Publishing Group Limited
2–4 Heron Quays
London E14 4JP

ISBN 0 600 60049 1

Printed in China

Notes

1 Standard level spoon measurements are used in all recipes.

1 tablespoon = one 15 ml spoon
1 teaspoon = one 5 ml spoon

2 Both imperial and metric measurements have been given in all recipes. Use one set of measurements only and not a mixture of both.

3 Measurements for canned food have been given as a standard metric equivalent.

4 Eggs should be medium unless otherwise stated. The Department of Health advises that eggs should not be consumed raw. This book contains dishes made with raw or lightly cooked eggs. It is prudent for more vulnerable people, such as pregnant and nursing mothers, invalids, the elderly, babies and young children, to avoid uncooked or lightly cooked dishes made with eggs. Once prepared, these dishes should be kept refrigerated and used promptly.

5 Milk should be full fat unless otherwise stated.

6 Poultry should be cooked thoroughly. To test if poultry is cooked, pierce the flesh through the thickest part with a skewer or fork – the juices should run clear, never pink or red.

7 Fresh herbs should be used unless otherwise stated. If unavailable, use dried herbs as an alternative, but halve the quantities stated.

8 Pepper should be freshly ground black pepper unless otherwise stated.

9 Ovens should be preheated to the specified temperature – if using a fan-assisted oven, follow the manufacturer's instructions for adjusting the time and the temperature.

10 This book includes dishes made with nuts and nut derivatives. It is advisable for customers with known allergic reactions to nuts and nut derivatives and those who may be potentially vulnerable to these allergies, such as pregnant and nursing mothers, invalids, the elderly, babies and children, to avoid dishes made with nuts and nut oils. It is also prudent to check the labels of pre-prepared ingredients for the possible inclusion of nut derivatives.

11 Vegetarians should look for the 'V' symbol on a cheese to ensure that it is made with vegetarian rennet. There are vegetarian forms of Parmesan, feta, Cheddar, Cheshire, Red Leicester, dolcelatte and many goats' cheeses, among others.

Fabulous soups and starters featuring fresh vegetables and seafood – all immensely, evocatively Italian.

The Mediterranean sea and many rivers supply an abundance of fish and seafood to inspire the Italian cook, whether preparing a substantial Spaghetti with Tuna for a family supper or mouthwatering Baked Trout Parcels for dinner guests.

Meat dishes, whether they are a sauce for pasta, a roast or a casserole, are prepared with herbs and spices. These are thoughtfully chosen to complement the meat, creating a range of tempting dishes.

Chicken is prepared in a wide variety of ways, reflecting the natural resources of the regions. Lemons, mushrooms, fennel, spinach and ham are among the many favourite Italian ingredients paired deliciously with poultry and game.

Because they are often served as a separate course, vegetables and salads are prepared with special care in Italy. Some of these dishes, such as Mushroom Lasagne, can also be served as a main course.

Although they are now served from New York to Sydney, nobody makes pizza so well as the Italians, in particular the Neapolitans.

Italians know how to end a meal with a flourish. Ices and cold desserts are favourites and fruit is often featured. Cakes and cheesecakes are popular, often featuring the creamy cheeses of Lombardy and Piedmont.

contents

introduction

To be strictly accurate, there is no such thing as Italian cooking. Rather, there are some twenty regional culinary styles, reflecting the fact that the separate provinces of Italy were not unified until 1861. Cooks continued to prepare food in the traditional ways of their region, based upon locally grown produce and other natural resources, and in many ways still continue to do so today.

The most obvious division is between the wealthier, fertile north and the poorer, sunnier south. Consequently, the ingredients that typify the cooking of Lombardy, for example – butter, rice, polenta, freshwater fish and veal – are not found in Calabrian dishes. Instead, these feature olive oil, a wealth of pasta, tomatoes and an abundance of citrus fruits. Every region has its own specialities. Neapolitans are credited with inventing pasta and are nicknamed *mangiamaccheroni* – pasta-eaters – by the Pugliesi, who, in turn, are dubbed *mangiafoglie* – leaf-eaters – because of their reputation for fine vegetable dishes. Bologna, capital of Emilia-Romagna, is known as *la grassa* – the fat – because of its generous use of cream and butter. This region also includes Parma, home to both Parmesan cheese and prosciutto di Parma, the classic dry-cured ham, and Modena, where balsamic vinegar originated. Tuscany, blessed with fertile plains, an abundant coastline and gentle hills, is rightly proud of its gastronomic reputation, earned by flavoursome soups, magnificent steaks and roasts, splendid fish and many bean dishes. Liguria is famous for its superb seafood and subtle use of spices, perhaps because the port of Genoa was the first to import them from the East. The soups, pot roasts and dumplings of Trentino betray its close proximity to the Austrian influences of the Tyrol. The Veneto is intensively farmed and the risottos and other rice dishes of Venice are nearly as well known as those of Milan. Fine seafood, especially in salads, is also a speciality of the region. Rome is the capital of Lazio as well as of Italy, so perhaps it is not surprising that the best cooking of all the other regions has found its way there, to be given a uniquely sophisticated twist. The far south of Italy and the islands of Sicily and Sardinia are probably best known for wonderfully rich desserts and deliciously sweet cakes and pastries, featuring honey, almonds and other nuts, figs, oranges, lemons and other fruits. Fish is plentiful and so, too, are olives and numerous vegetables, from aubergines to tomatoes.

What all these regions have in common is the use of the best quality, freshest seasonal ingredients. Italian housewives are among the fussiest in the world when they go to market. As a general rule, Italian cooking does not involve flamboyant sauces and wildly extravagant ingredients. On the contrary, it tends to be simple, although never dull, to allow the colour and texture and, above all, the flavour of the main ingredients to take the starring role.

'There is no sincerer love than the love of food.'

George Bernard Shaw

Pasta

There are at least 200 different pasta shapes, with three or four times as many names, and new ones are being developed all the time. Some names are standard, such as spaghetti, penne (quills) and orecchiette (little ears), but many names change from region to region.

All pasta is made from hard durum wheat flour, which has a high protein content. Pasta that incorporates egg is usually made into flat ribbons. Pasta may be coloured by a variety of added ingredients, such as spinach (green), tomato (red), beetroot (pink) and cuttlefish ink (black). There are no fixed rules about which shape should be served in any particular dish, although there are some useful guidelines. Pasta

shapes for soups are usually tiny, but larger shapes can be added to hearty soups, such as minestrone. Pasta for sauces can be divided into long flat noodles, such as tagliatelle, long thin noodles, such as spaghetti, hollow tubes, such as macaroni and chunky shapes, such as fusilli. The noodles are best suited to thinner sauces, while the chunkier pastas go with thicker, meaty sauces. Filled pasta, such as tortellini, is available from supermarkets, but fresh pasta for stuffing at home or homemade pasta dough allow a greater choice of fillings. Lasagne, flat sheets of pasta, is the most popular choice for baked dishes and can be used to make cannelloni.

While quite time-consuming, it is very satisfying to make pasta at home, once you have mastered the knack. If you are going to make it frequently, it might be worth investing in a pasta machine. Fresh filled pasta from a reliable delicatessen is worth buying, but unfilled pasta is usually as good dried as fresh.

To cook pasta, bring a large saucepan of lightly salted water to the boil. Add the pasta and start timing as soon as the water returns to the boil. Allow 8–12 minutes for dried unfilled pasta, 2–3 minutes for fresh unfilled pasta, 15–20 minutes for dried filled pasta and 8–10 minutes for fresh filled pasta. However, these are only guidelines and you should check frequently by biting a small piece. It should be tender, but still firm to the bite – what the Italians call *al dente*. Drain in a colander and toss immediately with a sauce, a knob of butter or a little olive oil.

fresh
homemade pasta dough

1 Mound the flour and salt on to a work surface. Make a well in the centre and add the eggs. Using your fingertips, draw the flour in from the sides and mix well. Add the olive oil and continue mixing to make a soft dough. Alternatively, process the ingredients in a food processor or blender to make a soft dough.

2 Turn the dough out on to a lightly floured surface and knead well until it is smooth and silky. Roll out the dough, giving it an occasional quarter-turn and stretching it out, until it resembles a thin sheet of cloth and is almost transparent.

3 Hang the pasta over the back of a chair or a broom handle and leave for about 10 minutes to dry. Alternatively, spread it on a table with one-third overhanging the end and keep turning it so that it dries out completely.

4 Roll the pasta up loosely like a Swiss roll and then cut through horizontally at regular intervals to make fettuccine (3 mm/⅛ inch) wide or tagliatelle (5 mm/¼ inch) wide. Unravel them and toss gently in a little flour. Leave them to dry on a cloth for at least 30 minutes before cooking in salted boiling water. Serve with a sauce or simply tossed with olive oil, garlic, salt and pepper and parsley.

300 g (10 oz) strong white plain flour, sifted, plus extra for dusting

pinch of salt

3 eggs

1 tablespoon olive oil

To Serve:

olive oil

finely chopped garlic

finely chopped parsley

salt and pepper

Serves 4

Preparation time: 30 minutes, plus drying

Cooking time: 2–3 minutes

minestrone ●

pumpkin soup ●

mixed antipasti ●

seafood salad ●

bruschetta with garlic, peppers & parmesan ●

spaghetti with carrot & courgette ribbons ●

gnocchi parcels with basil oil ●

green gnocchi ●

spinach & lemon risotto ●

onion savoury on italian bread ●

aubergines with lemon pesto ●

soups & starters

zuppe e antipasti

minestrone

1 Place the haricot beans in a large bowl and cover with water. Set aside to soak for 8 hours or overnight. Drain the beans and then rinse under cold running water.

2 Heat the oil in a large saucepan and add the onions, garlic and bacon. Sauté over a low heat, stirring occasionally, for about 5 minutes, until soft and golden brown.

3 Add the beans, water, marjoram, thyme and tomatoes, cover the pan and simmer for 2 hours. Add the carrots and simmer for 10 minutes. Stir in the potatoes and turnip and cook for a further 10 minutes.

4 Chop the celery and shred the cabbage. Add to the soup, together with the pasta shapes, and cook for 10 minutes, or until the pasta and all the vegetables are tender. Add the parsley and season to taste with salt and pepper. Stir in the Parmesan and then ladle into individual soup bowls. Serve immediately with extra Parmesan.

125 g (4 oz) dried haricot beans

3 tablespoons olive oil

2 onions, chopped

2 garlic cloves, crushed

2–3 rindless bacon rashers, chopped

1.8 litres (3 pints) water

1 teaspoon chopped marjoram

½ teaspoon chopped thyme

4 tomatoes, skinned, deseeded and chopped (see page 35)

2 carrots, diced

2 potatoes, diced

1 small turnip, diced

1–2 celery sticks

250 g (8 oz) cabbage

50 g (2 oz) small pasta shapes

1 tablespoon chopped parsley

3 tablespoons grated Parmesan cheese, plus extra to serve

salt and pepper

Serves 6

Preparation time: 20 minutes, plus soaking

Cooking time: about 2½ hours

■ You can use long-grain rice instead of the pasta shapes. Add it about 15 minutes before the end of the cooking time to ensure that it is tender.

pumpkin soup

1 Melt the butter or margarine in a large saucepan. Add the pumpkin. Stir well and cook over a low to moderate heat for 10 minutes. Add the warm water, the nutmeg and the thyme with salt and pepper to taste. Cover and cook quickly over a high heat until the pumpkin is soft.

2 Process the pumpkin mixture in a food processor or blender, with a little milk if necessary, until smooth. It may be necessary to do this in batches. Scrape the purée into a clean saucepan.

3 Add the remaining milk and the rice to the pumpkin purée in the pan. Stir well and cook, covered, for 30 minutes or until the rice is tender. Stir occasionally. Serve the soup in warmed bowls, garnished with croûtons.

50 g (2 oz) butter or margarine

750 g (1½ lb) pumpkin, peeled, deseeded and cut into large pieces

150 ml (¼ pint) warm water

¼ teaspoon grated nutmeg

pinch of dried thyme

1.5 litres (2½ pints) milk

50 g (2 oz) long-grain rice

salt and white pepper

croûtons, to garnish

Serves 6
Preparation time: about 10 minutes
Cooking time: 45 minutes

■ To make croûtons, cut the crusts off 50 g (2 oz) slices of day-old white bread and cut the bread into 5 mm (¼ inch) cubes. Heat 50 g (2 oz) butter in a heavy-based frying pan and sauté the bread cubes, stirring and tossing frequently, until golden. Drain well on kitchen paper.

mixed antipasti

1 Wrap 3–4 spears of asparagus in each slice of smoked salmon.

2 Arrange all the ingredients decoratively on a large serving platter. Season with salt and pepper and drizzle a little olive oil over the fish. Cover with clingfilm and refrigerate until required.

■ The original Italian name for this dish is *Antipasto Volente*. *Volente* is roughly translated to mean 'how it comes', so you can use any selection of seafood, sliced mozzarella cheese, Parma ham and salami. Slices of melon, sliced fresh figs, artichoke hearts, red peppers and olives could also be included.

250 g (8 oz) can asparagus spears

125 g (4 oz) or 4 slices of smoked salmon

200 g (7 oz) can tuna, drained

125 g (4 oz) can sardines

2 hard-boiled eggs, shelled and quartered

125–175 g (4–6 oz) cooked, peeled prawns

olive oil, for drizzling

salt and pepper

lemon wedges, to serve

Serves 4

Preparation time: 20 minutes

seafood salad

1 Soak the mussels in a bowl of cold water. Scrub them well to remove any barnacles and then remove the beards. Discard any that do not close when sharply tapped with a knife.

2 Put the mussels in a deep saucepan and add the water. Cover with a lid and steam over a high heat, shaking the pan occasionally, until the mussels open. Steam for 2 more minutes, then drain and set aside to cool. Discard any mussels that remain closed and remove the others from their shells.

3 Place the scallops, monkfish and squid on a large square of foil. Sprinkle with 2 tablespoons of the lemon juice, dot with the butter and scatter 1 tablespoon of the parsley over the top. Fold the foil over to form a parcel, seal the edges and cook in a preheated oven, 190°C (375°F), Gas Mark 5, for 20 minutes or until cooked.

4 Meanwhile, put the prawns in an ovenproof dish and sprinkle with garlic, 2 tablespoons of the lemon juice and 1 tablespoon of the parsley. Bake, uncovered, for 10 minutes. Arrange the cooked mussels, monkfish, scallops, squid and prawns in a serving dish and sprinkle the remaining lemon juice and the olive oil over the top. Season with salt and pepper to taste, sprinkle with the remaining parsley, allow to cool, then refrigerate until required.

500 g (1 lb) live mussels

125 ml (4 fl oz) water

8 scallops, shelled and sliced

375 g (12 oz) monkfish fillet, cubed

125 g (4 oz) prepared squid, sliced

8 tablespoons lemon juice

15 g (½ oz) butter

3 tablespoons finely chopped parsley

12 king prawns

2 garlic cloves, crushed

4 tablespoons olive oil

salt and pepper

Serves 4–6

Preparation time: 25 minutes, plus cooling and chilling

Cooking time: 25 minutes

bruschetta with garlic, peppers & parmesan

1 Heat a griddle pan and griddle all the peppers until the skins are charred. Peel the skin from the peppers, discard the seeds and roughly chop the flesh. Add the rosemary and half the Parmesan shavings. Season to taste with salt and pepper. Mix well with a little olive oil.

2 Toast the bread on both sides. Rub one side of the bread with the halved garlic cloves and drizzle with olive oil.

3 Place the prepared toast on a baking sheet, spoon the pepper mixture on to the bread and spread evenly. Sprinkle with the remaining Parmesan shavings and place under a preheated grill for a few minutes or until sizzling. Serve garnished with rosemary leaves.

4 red peppers

1 rosemary sprig, finely chopped

125 g (4 oz) Parmesan cheese, shaved

olive oil, for drizzling

4 large slices of country bread

2 garlic cloves, halved

salt and pepper

rosemary leaves, to garnish

Serves 4

Preparation time: 10 minutes

Cooking time: 15 minutes

1 Bring a large saucepan of lightly salted water to the boil. Add the spaghetti and cook until tender but still firm to the bite.

2 Meanwhile, using a vegetable peeler, slice the carrots and courgettes into long thin strips.

3 Melt the butter with the oil in a large frying pan. Add the garlic and carrots and sauté, stirring, for 5–7 minutes.

4 Drain the spaghetti and add to the pan with the courgette strips, basil, parsley, chives, marjoram and salt and pepper. Stir to mix and cook for 4–5 minutes until the courgettes are cooked through.

5 Remove the pan from the heat and transfer the spaghetti and vegetable mixture to a warmed serving dish. Add the shredded radicchio, toss to mix, sprinkle with the Parmesan shavings and serve immediately.

300 g (10 oz) spaghetti

3 carrots

3 courgettes

15 g (½ oz) butter

1 tablespoon olive oil

2 garlic cloves, crushed

75 g (3 oz) basil, finely chopped

40 g (1½ oz) parsley, chopped

25 g (1 oz) chives, snipped

2 tablespoons finely chopped marjoram

½ small radicchio, shredded

salt and pepper

Parmesan shavings, to garnish

Serves 4

Preparation time: 10 minutes

Cooking time: 14–17 minutes

spaghetti with carrot & courgette ribbons

18

gnocchi parcels with basil oil

1 Boil the potatoes until tender. Drain well and return to the pan to dry out over a gentle heat. Pass through a potato ricer, cool slightly, then work in the egg, salt, olive oil and enough flour to make a soft dough. Knead on a lightly floured surface then shape into a ball. Wrap in clingfilm and leave to rest while preparing the filling.

2 To make the filling, heat the oil in a small saucepan and gently sauté the garlic and shallot until soft but not browned. Purée with the tomatoes, ricotta and salt and pepper.

3 Knead the dough briefly, divide it into six pieces and roll out one piece thinly. Stamp out five 7 cm (3 inch) rounds with a pastry cutter and dampen the edges with water. Place a spoonful of filling in the centre of each one, fold it in half and press the edges together to seal. Repeat to make 30 parcels, place on a floured tray, cover and freeze for at least 2 hours.

4 To make the basil oil, pour boiling water over the basil leaves so they just wilt, refresh them under cold water and dry thoroughly. Purée the leaves with the oil and a little salt, to make a vibrant green sauce.

5 Plunge the frozen gnocchi into a large pan of lightly salted boiling water, return to boil and cook for 5–6 minutes, then drain well. Serve with basil oil and some Parmesan cheese and garnish with basil leaves.

475 g (15 oz) floury potatoes

1 large egg, beaten

1 teaspoon salt

1 tablespoon olive oil

175–185 g (6–6½) oz plain flour

basil leaves, to garnish

grated Parmesan cheese, to serve

Filling:

1 tablespoon olive oil

½ garlic clove, crushed

1 small shallot, finely chopped

50 g (2 oz) sun-dried tomatoes in oil, drained and chopped

150 g (5 oz) ricotta cheese

salt and pepper

Basil Oil:

50 g (2 oz) basil leaves

8 tablespoons extra virgin olive oil

pinch of salt

Serves 6

Preparation time: 40 minutes, plus freezing

Cooking time: about 30 minutes

1 Place the spinach and half of the butter in a pan and cook until the spinach is very tender and looks as if it is about to stick to the pan. Add the ricotta and cook for a further 3 minutes.

2 Add the drained bread mixture and eggs and mix well to a firm, but not too dry mixture. Season with salt and pepper. If the mixture appears a little too soft, add a little flour or dried breadcrumbs to absorb the excess moisture. Roll into pointed sausage shapes about 2.5 cm (1 inch) in length and place on a board to dry for 1 hour.

3 Cook the gnocchi, in batches, in salted boiling water for about 4 minutes until they rise to the surface. Remove with a slotted spoon and place in a warmed serving dish. Add the remaining butter and toss well to coat. Sprinkle with the Parmesan. Garnish with lime or lemon slices, if using, and serve immediately.

500 g (1 lb) spinach leaves, drained and finely chopped

125 g (4 oz) butter

175 g (6 oz) ricotta cheese

200 g (7 oz) day-old bread, soaked in 500 ml (17 fl oz) milk and drained

2 eggs

a little flour or dried breadcrumbs

50 g (2 oz) Parmesan cheese, grated

salt and pepper

lime or lemon slices, to garnish (optional)

Serves 6

Preparation time: 20 minutes, plus drying

Cooking time: 12–15 minutes

green gnocchi

spinach & lemon risotto

1 Heat the stock in a saucepan to a gentle simmer.

2 Melt 50 g (2 oz) of the butter and the olive oil in a saucepan, add the shallots and sauté for 3 minutes.

3 Add the rice and stir well to coat the grains thoroughly with butter and oil. Add a ladleful of stock, enough to cover the rice, and stir well. Simmer gently and continue to stir as frequently as possible, adding more stock as each ladleful is absorbed.

4 Before you add the last of the stock, stir in the chopped spinach, lemon rind and juice and season to taste with salt and pepper. Increase the heat, stir well then add the remaining stock and butter. Cook for a few minutes, then add half of the Parmesan and mix in well. Serve garnished with the remaining Parmesan and extra lemon rind.

1 litre (1¾ pints) chicken or vegetable stock

125 g (4 oz) butter

1 tablespoon olive oil

2 shallots, finely chopped

300 g (10 oz) risotto rice

500 g (1 lb) baby spinach, chopped

grated rind and juice of 1 lemon

125 g (4 oz) Parmesan cheese, grated

salt and pepper

grated lemon rind, to garnish

Serves 4
Preparation time: 10 minutes
Cooking time: 20–25 minutes

■ The secrets of making risotto are to use a proper risotto rice, such as arborio, which absorbs a great deal of cooking liquid without becoming too soft, and to stir the rice as often as you can while it is cooking. Do not attempt to reheat a risotto, as it will become heavy.

onion savoury on italian bread

1 Put the onions in a bowl, cover with cold water and soak overnight.

2 Heat the oil in a large, heavy-based pan, add the bacon and fry gently until browned. Drain the onions thoroughly, then add to the pan with the basil and season to taste with salt and pepper. Cook over a low heat for 20 minutes, stirring occasionally.

3 Add the tomatoes, cover the pan, lower the heat and cook very gently for 10 minutes. Taste and adjust the seasoning. Beat the eggs and Parmesan together, then add to the pan. Remove from the heat immediately and stir vigorously.

4 Put a slice of hot toast in each warmed soup bowl, then spoon over the hot savoury. Serve immediately, garnished with basil.

750 g (1½ lb) onions, sliced

2 tablespoons olive oil

125 g (4 oz) bacon, chopped

a few basil leaves, torn

375 g (12 oz) tomatoes, skinned and mashed

3 eggs, beaten

75 g (3 oz) Parmesan cheese, grated

4 slices of hot toasted ciabatta or focaccia bread

salt and pepper

basil leaves, shredded, to garnish

Serves 4
Preparation time: 20 minutes, plus soaking
Cooking time: 35 minutes

aubergines with lemon pesto

1 Heat a griddle pan. Place the aubergines on the griddle and cook for 3 minutes on each side, then remove and arrange them on a warmed serving dish. Repeat until all the aubergines are cooked.

2 To make the lemon pesto, place the basil, pine nuts, garlic, Parmesan, lemon rind and juice and olive oil in a food processor or blender and season to taste with salt and pepper. Process until smooth.

3 Drizzle the lemon pesto over the aubergines and serve with crusty bread.

4 aubergines, cut into rounds, or baby aubergines, sliced lengthways

Lemon Pesto:

1 large bunch of basil

75 g (3 oz) pine nuts, toasted

1 garlic clove

75 g (3 oz) Parmesan cheese, grated

grated rind of 2 lemons

4 tablespoons lemon juice

3 tablespoons olive oil

salt and pepper

crusty bread, to serve

Serves 4
Preparation time: 10 minutes,
Cooking time: about 20 minutes

cod baked with potatoes, onions & tomatoes •

fresh tuna with tomatoes •

swordfish palermo-style •

baked trout parcels •

mediterranean fish steaks •

red mullet with tomatoes •

tagliatelle with shellfish & broccoli •

spaghetti with tuna •

spaghetti with sardines, anchovies & fennel •

mussels with peppers •

fish & seafood
frutti di mare

cod baked with potatoes, onions & tomatoes

1 Cook the potatoes in boiling salted water until almost done. Cut them into thick slices and coat them in olive oil. Arrange them around the edge of a greased ovenproof dish and place the fish in the centre.

2 Heat the olive oil in a frying pan, add the onion and sauté gently for about 5 minutes until soft. Add the garlic and oregano and cook for 2–3 minutes. Add the tomatoes, wine or stock and season to taste with salt and pepper and simmer for a few minutes.

3 Spoon half of the tomato mixture over the fish and potatoes in the ovenproof dish. Mix the remaining tomato mixture in a small bowl with the breadcrumbs and cheese and then pour over the fish. Bake in a preheated oven, 200°C (400°F), Gas Mark 6, for 15 minutes or until the fish is cooked. Sprinkle with the chopped parsley and serve immediately.

12 small new potatoes

1 tablespoon olive oil, extra for coating

4 cod fillets

2 tablespoons extra virgin olive oil

2 onions, finely chopped

1 garlic clove, crushed

1 tablespoon chopped oregano

400 g (13 oz) can chopped tomatoes

125 ml (4 fl oz) dry white wine or fish stock

75 g (3 oz) fine breadcrumbs

50 g (2 oz) Parmesan cheese, grated

salt and pepper

chopped parsley, to garnish

Serves 4

Preparation time: 15 minutes

Cooking time: 45 minutes

■ Although cod is not a Mediterranean fish, so many of the ingredients in this recipe, such as tomatoes, oregano and Parmesan, are typically Italian that the end result is a delicious melange of Italian flavours.

fresh tuna with tomatoes

1 Wash the tuna steaks and pat dry with kitchen paper. Season with plenty of salt and pepper, then dust the steaks lightly with flour. Heat half of the olive oil in a large shallow frying pan and sauté the tuna steaks until golden on each side. Carefully remove them from the pan, transfer to a dish and keep warm.

2 Heat the remaining oil in the pan, add the onion and garlic and sauté for about 3 minutes until soft and golden. Add the tomatoes, parsley, basil, bay leaf and mashed anchovies and stir well. Heat through gently, allowing the tomatoes to keep their shape.

3 Return the tuna to the pan, season to taste with salt and pepper and simmer gently for 15 minutes, turning once. Turn off the heat, add the olives and leave to stand for 5 minutes. To serve, discard the bay leaf and serve the tuna steaks on the bed of vegetables.

4 x 150 g (5 oz) tuna steaks

flour, for dusting

3 tablespoons olive oil

1 onion, chopped

2 garlic cloves, crushed

750 g (1½ lb) tomatoes, skinned and chopped

2 tablespoons chopped parsley

a few basil leaves, chopped

1 bay leaf

4 anchovy fillets, mashed

8 black olives

salt and pepper

Serves 4

Preparation time: 15 minutes

Cooking time: 30 minutes

swordfish palermo-style

1 Wash the swordfish steaks and pat them dry with kitchen paper. Sprinkle them with salt and then dust lightly with flour on both sides.

2 Heat the oil in a heavy–based frying pan. Add the garlic cloves and fry over a low heat until golden. Remove and discard the garlic. Add the swordfish steaks to the pan and cook, turning once, until browned on both sides. Remove and keep warm.

3 Add the anchovies and onion to the pan and fry until golden and the anchovies have reduced to a purée. Add the tomatoes and rosemary and simmer over a low heat for 30 minutes, until thickened.

4 Add the olives and capers and season to taste with salt and pepper. Return the swordfish to the sauce and then heat through gently. Serve garnished with the rosemary.

4 x 250 g (8 oz) swordfish steaks

flour, for dusting

125 ml (4 fl oz) olive oil

2 garlic cloves

4 canned anchovy fillets, drained and finely chopped

1 onion, finely chopped

4 tomatoes, skinned, deseeded and chopped (see page 35)

pinch of dried rosemary, crumbled

12 green olives, pitted and sliced

1 tablespoon capers

salt and pepper

2 tablespoons chopped rosemary, to garnish

Serves 4

Preparation time: 15 minutes

Cooking time: 45 minutes

baked trout parcels

1 Heat the olive oil in a frying pan. Add the garlic, onion and celery and fry over a fairly low heat for about 10 minutes, until soft and golden. Add 2 rosemary sprigs and the white wine and season to taste with salt and pepper. Cook for 5 minutes.

2 Cut out 2 double sheets of greaseproof paper large enough to enclose the trout. Brush the paper lightly with a little oil. Divide the onion mixture equally between the 2 pieces of paper.

3 Wash the trout and dry well with kitchen paper. Sprinkle inside and out with salt and pepper. Place a trout on top of the onion mixture on each piece of greaseproof paper and top with a sprig of rosemary.

4 Fold the paper over the fish and wrap loosely, securing the sides with a double fold and double folding the ends. Place on a baking sheet and cook in a preheated oven, 180°C (350°F), Gas Mark 4, for 20 minutes, until the fish is cooked and tender. Remove the trout from the paper and serve garnished with sprigs of rosemary.

2 tablespoons olive oil

2 garlic cloves, crushed

1 onion, chopped

1 celery stick, chopped

4 rosemary sprigs, plus extra to garnish

2 tablespoons dry white wine

2 x 375 g (12 oz) trout, cleaned

salt and pepper

Serves 2
Preparation time: 10–15 minutes
Cooking time: 35 minutes

mediterranean fish steaks

1 Heat the oil in a frying pan. Add the onions and garlic and fry until softened. Add the green pepper rings and continue frying for 3 minutes. Remove from the heat and place half the mixture in a casserole.

2 Arrange half the tomato slices on top, sprinkle with half the basil and season to taste with salt and pepper. Place the fish steaks on top, sprinkle with the lemon juice and add the remaining tomato slices, basil, onion and green pepper mixture. Pour in the wine.

3 Cover and cook in a preheated oven, 180°C (350°F), Gas Mark 4, for about 45 minutes, or until the fish is tender. Serve garnished with basil sprigs.

4 tablespoons olive oil

2 onions, thinly sliced

1 garlic clove, finely chopped

1 green pepper, cored, deseeded and sliced into rings

4 large tomatoes, skinned and sliced (see page 35)

2 teaspoons dried basil

4 x 150 g (5 oz) white fish steaks

2 teaspoons lemon juice

6 tablespoons dry white wine

salt and pepper

basil sprigs, to garnish

Serves 4

Preparation time: 10 minutes

Cooking time: 1 hour

red mullet with tomatoes

1 Heat 2 tablespoons of the oil in a pan and cook the onion and garlic gently until lightly browned. Add the anchovy fillets, tomatoes, white wine, bay leaf and thyme. Season to taste with salt and pepper and cook gently until the sauce thickens.

2 Meanwhile, heat 4–6 tablespoons of the oil in a frying pan. Season the flour with salt and pepper, and coat the fish with the flour. Fry until golden brown on one side, then turn carefully and cook on the second side.

3 Add the sauce to the pan with the red mullet and cook for a further 6–8 minutes. Transfer the fish carefully to a warmed serving dish. Toss the olives in the sauce and heat through. Remove the bay leaf and pour the sauce over the fish. Sprinkle the thyme on top and serve hot.

6–8 tablespoons olive oil

1 onion, finely chopped

1 garlic clove, crushed

2–3 anchovy fillets, chopped

400 g (13 oz) can chopped tomatoes

150 ml (¼ pint) dry white wine

1 bay leaf

¼ teaspoon chopped thyme

4 tablespoons plain flour

4 x 175–250 g (6–8 oz) red mullet, scales and fins removed

12 black olives, pitted

salt and pepper

thyme sprigs, to garnish

Serves 4
Preparation time: 15–20 minutes
Cooking time: 30–35 minutes

tagliatelle with shellfish & broccoli

1 Break the broccoli into small florets and cook in boiling water for 3 minutes. Drain and set aside.

2 Heat the oil in a large heavy-based pan. Add the onion and garlic and fry over a medium heat until softened. Stir in the mushrooms, scallops, prawns and vermouth. Bring to the boil and cook until only about 2 tablespoons of the vermouth remain. Add the cream, parsley, marjoram and broccoli and season to taste with salt and pepper.

3 Meanwhile, cook the tagliatelle in lightly salted boiling water until tender but still firm to the bite. Drain and place in a warmed serving dish. Pour over the shellfish and broccoli sauce and serve immediately with grated pecorino cheese.

375 g (12 oz) broccoli

2 tablespoons olive oil

1 onion, chopped

1 garlic clove, crushed

125 g (4 oz) button mushrooms, sliced

250 g (8 oz) shelled scallops

175 g (6 oz) cooked, peeled prawns

150 ml (¼ pint) dry vermouth

300 ml (½ pint) double cream

1 tablespoon chopped parsley

1 teaspoon chopped marjoram

375 g (12 oz) dried tagliatelle verde

salt and pepper

grated pecorino cheese, to serve

Serves 4–6

Preparation time: 10 minutes

Cooking time: 20 minutes

spaghetti
with tuna

1 Heat the oil in a heavy-based pan. Add the garlic and cook, stirring occasionally, until golden brown. Add the tomatoes and herbs and season to taste with pepper. Bring to the boil and simmer, uncovered, for 30 minutes until thickened. Add the tuna, anchovy essence and capers, if using.

2 Meanwhile, cook the spaghetti in lightly salted boiling water until tender but still firm to the bite. Drain well, turn into a warmed serving dish, add the butter and toss.

3 Taste the sauce and add salt if necessary, then spoon it over the pasta. Garnish with oregano or basil, if using, and serve immediately.

■ The easiest way to skin tomatoes is to cut a cross in the base and then drop them in boiling water for 30 seconds. Drain and cool. The skins will then slide off easily.

4 tablespoons olive oil

2–3 garlic cloves, crushed

1 kg (2 lb) tomatoes, skinned, deseeded and chopped (see below)

1 tablespoon chopped basil

1 tablespoon chopped oregano

400 g (13 oz) canned tuna, drained and flaked

1 teaspoon anchovy essence

2 teaspoons capers (optional)

500 g (1 lb) fresh spaghetti

25 g (1 oz) butter

salt and pepper

oregano or basil sprigs, to garnish (optional)

Serves 4–6

Preparation time: 15 minutes

Cooking time: 35 minutes

spaghetti with sardines, anchovies & fennel

1 Cook the fennel in boiling salted water until almost tender. Drain well, reserving the cooking liquid. Chop the fennel coarsely.

2 Heat 3 tablespoons of the oil in a pan and add the garlic. Cook until golden brown then add the sardines and cook for a further 10 minutes.

3 Meanwhile, heat another 3 tablespoons of the oil in a pan and cook the onions until they are soft and brown. Add the fennel, sultanas, pine nuts, anchovies, parsley and wine or fish stock. Season with salt and pepper. Cook over a moderate heat for 10 minutes.

4 Cook the spaghetti in boiling salted water to which the fennel water has been added until tender but still firm to the bite. Drain well and place half in an oven-to-table dish. Cover with half the sardines and a little of the onions and fennel.

5 Repeat the layers and sprinkle breadcrumbs and a little oil over the top. Cook in a preheated oven, 200°C (400°F), Gas Mark 6, for 20 minutes. Serve immediately.

1 head fennel, quartered

8–10 tablespoons olive oil

2 garlic cloves, crushed

500 g (1 lb) sardines

2 large onions, finely sliced

1 tablespoon sultanas

1 tablespoon pine nuts

6 anchovy fillets, chopped

2 tablespoons chopped parsley

150 ml (5 fl oz) white wine or fish stock

500 g (1 lb) spaghetti

white breadcrumbs, lightly browned

salt and pepper

Serves 4

Preparation time: 10 minutes

Cooking time: 1 hour

mussels with peppers

1 Soak the mussels in a bowl of cold water. Scrub them well to remove any barnacles and then remove the beards. Discard any that do not close when sharply tapped with a knife.

2 Heat the butter and oil in a shallow, flameproof casserole. Add the celery and peppers and fry until softened. Add the garlic, lemon rind, bay leaf, mussels and wine. Season to taste with salt and pepper.

3 Cover and cook over a high heat, shaking the pan constantly, for 2–3 minutes. Remove the opened mussels, cover the pan and cook for 1 minute. Discard any mussels which have not opened. Drain and reserve the liquid from the casserole. Pull off and discard the empty top shell from each mussel. Return the mussels to the casserole, and sprinkle with the breadcrumbs.

4 Beat together the eggs, cream, 6 tablespoons of the reserved cooking liquid and the turmeric and season to taste with salt and pepper. Pour over the mussels and scatter the cheese on top. Cook in a preheated oven, 200°C (400°F), Gas Mark 6, for 10–15 minutes, until set and golden. Serve immediately, garnished with tomato quarters.

2 kg (4 lb) live mussels

25 g (1 oz) butter

2 tablespoons olive oil

4 celery sticks, sliced

1 red pepper, cored, deseeded and diced

1 yellow pepper, cored, deseeded and diced

2 garlic cloves, crushed

5 cm (2 inch) strip of lemon rind

1 bay leaf

6 tablespoons dry white wine

125 g (4 oz) fresh white breadcrumbs

4 eggs

2 tablespoons single cream

¼ teaspoon ground turmeric

2 tablespoons grated Parmesan cheese

salt and pepper

tomato quarters, to garnish

Serves 4

Preparation time: 20 minutes

Cooking time: 20–25 minutes

meat

carne

spaghetti alla bolognese

1 First make the meat sauce. Heat the oil in a saucepan or deep frying pan and sauté the onion, garlic, bacon, carrot and celery until soft and golden. Add the beef and cook, stirring occasionally, until browned. Add the red wine and bring to the boil. Reduce the heat slightly and cook over a moderate heat until most of the wine has evaporated. Season to taste with salt and pepper.

2 Add the milk and a little grated nutmeg, stir well and cook until the milk has been absorbed by the meat mixture. Add the tomatoes, sugar and oregano. Reduce the heat to a gentle simmer and cook, uncovered, for at least 1 hour, stirring occasionally, until the sauce is reduced and richly coloured.

3 Bring a large saucepan of lightly salted water to the boil, add the spaghetti and cook until tender but still firm to the bite. Drain well and season with pepper. Pour the sauce over the spaghetti and sprinkle with the Parmesan cheese.

■ Many people think that this famous sauce, or ragú, from the central city of Bologna, should be served with spaghetti, but tagliatelle is also authentic.

500 g (1 lb) spaghetti

salt and pepper

50 g (2 oz) grated Parmesan cheese, to serve

Meat Sauce:

4 tablespoons olive oil

1 onion, finely chopped

1 garlic clove, crushed

4 streaky bacon rashers, rinded and chopped

1 carrot, diced

1 celery stick, diced

500 g (1 lb) lean minced beef

150 ml (¼ pint) red wine

125 ml (4 fl oz) milk

grated nutmeg

400 g (13 oz) can chopped tomatoes

1 tablespoon sugar

1 tablespoon chopped oregano

salt and pepper

Serves 4

Preparation time: about 20 minutes

Cooking time: about 1½ hours

1 Heat the oil in a pan. Add the veal and fry, stirring frequently, until it is golden brown. Remove from the pan with a slotted spoon and set aside on a plate. Add the onion and carrot to the pan and cook until lightly coloured. Return the veal to the pan, together with the wine and stock. Season lightly with salt and pepper and simmer over a low heat for 40–45 minutes, until the meat is tender.

2 Remove the meat and vegetables from the pan with a slotted spoon and purée in a food processor or blender with the chicken. Stir in the chopped spinach. Boil the liquid until it has reduced to about 2 tablespoons. Stir into the meat and spinach with sufficient cream to soften the mixture.

3 Pipe or spoon the filling into the cannelloni tubes. Place the filled cannelloni in a buttered ovenproof dish and cover with the tomato sauce. Bake in a preheated oven, 190°C (375°F), Gas Mark 5, for 40–45 minutes. Sprinkle a little Parmesan over the top 5 minutes before the end of the cooking time and serve the rest separately.

1–2 tablespoons olive oil

375 g (12 oz) lean stewing veal, diced

1 onion, sliced

1 carrot, sliced

150 ml (¼ pint) dry white wine

300 ml (½ pint) chicken stock

125 g (4 oz) cooked chicken

125 g (4 oz) cooked spinach, chopped

2–3 tablespoons double cream

12 no-precook cannelloni tubes

2 quantities Tomato Sauce (see page 68)

40 g (1½ oz) Parmesan cheese, grated

salt and pepper

Serves 4

Preparation time: 20–30 minutes

Cooking time: 1½ hours

meat-filled cannelloni

chilli pasta with pancetta

1 Heat the oil in a saucepan and fry the shallots and pancetta gently for 6–8 minutes until golden. Add the chilli flakes and chopped tomatoes, half cover the pan and simmer for 20 minutes until the sauce is thick and has reduced. Season to taste with salt and pepper.

2 Meanwhile, bring at least 2 litres (3½ pints) of water to the boil in a large saucepan. Add a pinch of salt. Cook the pasta until tender but still firm to the bite.

3 To make the garlic crumbs, put the bread in a food processor and reduce to crumbs. Heat the butter in a frying pan, add the garlic and bread-crumbs and stir-fry until golden and crisp. (Don't let the crumbs catch and burn or the dish will be ruined.)

4 To serve, toss the cooked pasta with the tomato sauce and sprinkle each serving with some of the garlic crumbs. Garnish with the parsley sprigs.

3 tablespoons olive oil

2 shallots, finely chopped

8 slices unsmoked pancetta, chopped

2 teaspoons crushed chilli flakes

500 g (1 lb) canned chopped tomatoes

500–750 g (1–1½ lb) pasta shells

salt and pepper

flat leaf parsley leaves, to garnish

Garlic Crumbs:

6 slices white bread, crusts removed

125 g (4 oz) butter

2 garlic cloves, finely chopped

Serves 4–6

Preparation time: 5 minutes

Cooking time: about 30 minutes

loin of lamb with blue cheese & polenta

1 Heat a griddle pan and sear the loins all over for about 10–12 minutes. Transfer them to a lightly oiled roasting tin and cook in a preheated oven, 200°C (400°F), Gas Mark 6, for 10–15 minutes for rare meat and 20–25 minutes for well done.

2 Meanwhile, bring the water to the boil in a saucepan, add the polenta and mix well. Simmer, stirring, for 10 minutes until the polenta thickens and the water is absorbed. Add the butter, dolcelatte and mascarpone torte and marjoram and season to taste with salt and pepper. Mix well and keep warm.

3 Leave the lamb to rest for 5 minutes. Serve in slices, with the polenta and garnished with sage sprigs.

2 loins of lamb, about 1.25 kg (2½ lb), boned and rolled

vegetable oil

1 litre (1¾ pints) water

175 g (6 oz) polenta

75 g (3 oz) butter

175 g (6 oz) dolcelatte and mascarpone torte

3 tablespoons chopped marjoram

sea salt flakes and pepper

sage sprigs, to garnish

Serves 6

Preparation time: 15 minutes

Cooking time: about 45 minutes

risi e bisi

1 Heat two-thirds of the butter in a pan. Add the bacon and fry until lightly coloured. Add the onion and cook until soft, but not coloured. Stir in the chopped parsley and the peas. Add a pinch of sugar, season lightly with salt and pepper and cook for 3 minutes. If using fresh peas, pour in half the stock and cook over a low heat for 10–15 minutes. If using frozen peas, add all the stock to the pan and bring to the boil.

2 Add the rice and mix together well. Season and simmer for 10–15 minutes, until the rice is just tender. If necessary, add a little more stock or some water to keep the risotto moist. When the rice is cooked, check the seasoning and stir in the remaining butter and the Parmesan. Pile into a warmed serving dish and serve hot.

75 g (3 oz) butter

125 g (4 oz) piece rindless streaky bacon, diced

1 large onion, chopped

1 tablespoon chopped parsley

425 g (14 oz) shelled or frozen peas

pinch of sugar

1.2 litres (2 pints) chicken stock

375 g (12 oz) arborio rice

50–75 g (2–3 oz) Parmesan cheese, grated

salt and pepper

Serves 2
Preparation time: 10 minutes
Cooking time: 35–40 minutes

■ Arborio is the best quality risotto rice, with a rounder grain than long-grain rice. It can absorb a lot of liquid and gives risotto its characteristic creamy texture.

veal chops with gremolata

1 Coat both sides of the veal chops with seasoned flour. Melt the butter and oil in a flameproof casserole, add the chops and brown well on each side. Remove from the casserole and keep warm.

2 Add the onions, garlic, celery and carrot to the pan and sauté for 3 minutes. Add the bay leaves, tomatoes, stock and wine and season to taste with salt and pepper. Mix well and bring to the boil. Return the chops to the casserole and turn to coat them in the sauce. Cover and cook in a preheated oven, 200°C (400°F), Gas Mark 6, for 20 minutes.

3 While the chops are cooking, make the gremolata. Mix together the parsley, sage, lemon rind and garlic.

4 Transfer the chops to a warmed serving platter and keep them warm. Boil the sauce to reduce if necessary, then pour it over the chops and spoon some of the gremolata over each one.

4 thin veal chops

75 g (3 oz) seasoned flour

50 g (2 oz) butter

1 tablespoon olive oil

2 onions, chopped

2 garlic cloves, crushed

2 celery sticks, chopped

1 carrot, chopped

2 bay leaves

6 tomatoes, skinned, deseeded and chopped (see page 35)

125 ml (4 fl oz) chicken stock

125 ml (4 fl oz) white wine

salt and pepper

Gremolata:

2 tablespoons finely chopped parsley

1 tablespoon finely chopped sage

rind of 3 lemons, finely grated

3 large garlic cloves, chopped

Serves 4

Preparation time: 15 minutes

Cooking time: 25 minutes

paprika lamb

1 Mix together the marinade ingredients in a non–metallic dish and season to taste with salt and pepper. Place the chops in the marinade, turn to coat, and set aside for about 2–3 hours.

2 Drain the chops and pat dry with kitchen paper. Place them in a shallow ovenproof dish. Sprinkle the onion over the chops and cover with foil. Cook in a preheated oven, 190°C (375°F), Gas Mark 5, for 1 hour.

3 Mix the yogurt with the paprika and spoon over the chops. Continue cooking for 15 minutes. Serve sprinkled with paprika and garnished with parsley.

4 lamb chops

1 onion, finely chopped

150 ml (¼ pint) natural yogurt

2 tablespoons paprika

Marinade:

2 tablespoons white wine

2 teaspoons lemon juice

½ teaspoon sugar

½ teaspoon dried thyme

salt and pepper

To Garnish:

paprika

parsley sprigs

Serves 4
Preparation time: 5 minutes, plus marinating
Cooking time: 1¼ hours

■ Although much less spicy than chilli and cayenne, paprika may be hot or mild. Check the label when buying it.

italian lamb with rosemary oil

1 Make small incisions with a sharp knife all over the lamb fillets and insert the garlic slivers and rosemary sprigs. Heat a griddle pan and cook the fillets, turning occasionally, until charred all over, about 20 minutes for rare meat, or 30–40 minutes for well done. Add the onions for the last few minutes and char on the outside.

2 Place the chopped rosemary and the oil in a mortar and crush with a pestle to release the flavours. Season to taste with salt and pepper. Allow the lamb to rest for 5 minutes then carve into slices. Spoon the rosemary oil over the top and serve immediately with the griddled onions. Serve with fresh pasta, lightly tossed in olive oil, and Parmesan shavings.

2 lamb fillets, trimmed of fat, weighing 750 g (1½ lb)

4 garlic cloves, cut into slivers

a few small rosemary sprigs

2 red onions, quartered

1 tablespoon chopped rosemary

4 tablespoons olive oil

salt and pepper

To Serve:

fresh pasta

Parmesan cheese shavings

Serves 4
Preparation time: 20 minutes
Cooking time: 20–40 minutes

1 Rub the beef all over with salt and pepper. Heat the oil in a flameproof casserole, add the beef and brown on all sides, then remove from the casserole.

2 Add the onion, garlic, carrots and celery to the casserole and fry until the onion is softened. Stir in the tomatoes, wine, oregano and bay leaf and bring to the boil.

3 Return the beef to the casserole and turn over in the liquid. Cover tightly and cook in a preheated oven, 180°C (350°F), Gas Mark 4, for 3 hours or until the meat is tender. Baste occasionally during the cooking.

4 Remove the beef from the casserole, place on a warmed serving plate and keep hot.

5 Boil the cooking liquid on top of the stove until well reduced and thickened. Strain and serve as a sauce, with the beef.

1–1.25 kg (2–3 lb) piece of beef topside

3 tablespoons olive oil

1 onion, chopped

1 garlic clove, crushed

2 large carrots, sliced

2 celery sticks, sliced

250 g (8 oz) can chopped tomatoes

300 ml (½ pint) dry red wine

1 teaspoon dried oregano

1 bay leaf

salt and pepper

Serves 4

Preparation time: 10 minutes

Cooking time: 3¼ hours

italian pot roast

prosciutto & tomato fettucine

1 Heat the oil in a pan, and gently fry the onion for 3 minutes. Add the prosciutto and cook for a further 2–3 minutes.

2 Add the garlic, chilli and tomatoes, and season to taste with salt and pepper. Cook gently for 10 minutes until thickened.

3 Cook the pasta in boiling salted water until tender but firm to the bite. This will take about 3 minutes for fresh pasta and 10–15 minutes for dried. Drain and toss with the sauce and grated pecorino. Transfer to a heated serving dish and serve immediately.

4 tablespoon olive oil

1 onion, finely chopped

125 g/4 oz prosciutto, diced

2 garlic cloves, crushed

1 fresh chilli, deseeded and finely chopped

750 g/1½ lb tomatoes, skinned (see page 35) and chopped

500 g/1 lb fettuccine or tagliatelle (fresh or dried)

salt and pepper

75 g/3 oz pecorino cheese, freshly grated, to serve

Serves 4

Preparation time: 15 minutes

Cooking time: about 20–35 minutes

■ Pecorino Romano is a hard, grating cheese not dissimilar to Parmesan. It has been made for two thousand years in southern Italy. The main ingredient is sheep's milk.

pappardelle with chicken liver ragù •

chicken & ham cannelloni •

lemon chicken •

chicken with wild mushrooms •

chicken with ham & fennel •

turkey breasts with parmesan, egg & spinach •

poussins medici •

quails with peas & gammon •

creamy chicken livers with port •

poultry & game

pollame e selvaggina

pappardelle with chicken liver ragù

1 Heat the oil in a heavy-based saucepan, add the pancetta and onion and cook, stirring, over a moderate heat until the pancetta starts to crispen. Add the minced beef and cook for a few minutes until it changes colour, stirring and pressing it constantly to break up any lumps. Add half of the hot stock, then the tomatoes, wine, tomato purée, garlic, sage and salt and pepper. Bring to the boil, then lower the heat, partially cover the pan and simmer gently for 30 minutes, stirring occasionally.

2 Add the chicken livers and the remaining stock. Stir well then cook for another 30 minutes.

3 Towards the end of cooking, plunge the pasta into a large saucepan of lightly salted boiling water and simmer for 2–3 minutes until tender but still firm to the bite. Drain thoroughly then transfer to a large serving bowl.

4 Taste the sauce and adjust the seasoning if necessary. Pour the sauce over the pasta and toss quickly to mix. Serve immediately, sprinkled with Parmesan cheese.

2 tablespoons olive oil

125 g (4 oz) pancetta, finely diced

1 onion, finely chopped

250 g (8 oz) minced beef

450 ml (¾ pint) hot beef stock

400 g (13 oz) can chopped plum tomatoes

150 ml (¼ pint) red or white wine

1 tablespoon tomato purée

1 garlic clove, crushed

1 teaspoon dried sage

125 g (4 oz) frozen chicken livers, defrosted and diced

300 g (10 oz) fresh pappardelle

salt and pepper

grated Parmesan cheese, to serve

Serves 6–8

Preparation time: 20 minutes

Cooking time: 1¼ hours

chicken & ham cannelloni

1 First prepare the sauce. Heat the oil in a saucepan. Add the onion and garlic and cook over a moderate heat until soft but not brown. Add all the remaining ingredients and bring to the boil, stirring occasionally. Lower the heat, cover and simmer for 40 minutes.

2 To make the filling, heat the oil in a frying pan. Add the onion and fry over a moderate heat until soft but not brown. Add the chicken and cook for a few minutes, until just done. Remove from the heat. Stir in the ham and soft cheese and season to taste with salt and pepper. Mix well and use to fill the cannelloni tubes.

3 Place the filled cannelloni in a lightly greased ovenproof dish, pour over the prepared tomato sauce and sprinkle with the Parmesan. Bake in the centre of a preheated oven, 190°C (375°F), Gas Mark 5, for 40 minutes. Serve immediately, garnished with parsley sprigs.

1 tablespoon olive oil

1 small onion, finely chopped

175 g (6 oz) boneless, skinless chicken, minced

125 g (4 oz) lean ham, finely chopped

65 g (2½ oz) full-fat soft cheese with garlic and herbs

8 no-precook cannelloni tubes

3 tablespoons grated Parmesan cheese

salt and pepper

flat leaf parsley sprigs, to garnish

Tomato Sauce:

1 tablespoon olive oil

1 large onion, finely chopped

2 garlic cloves, crushed

400 g (13 oz) can chopped tomatoes

2 teaspoons sugar

3 tablespoons tomato purée

150 ml (¼ pint) chicken stock

1 teaspoon dried mixed herbs

Serves 4
Preparation time: 30 minutes
Cooking time: 1½ hours

lemon
chicken

1 Using a sharp knife and kitchen
scissors, cut the chicken into
8 joints and put them into a shallow
ovenproof dish.

2 Squeeze the juice from the
lemons into a small bowl. Reserve
the lemon skins.

3 Crush 2 of the garlic cloves and
add them to the lemon juice with
the chilli and the honey. Stir well, then
pour this marinade over the chicken
pieces and tuck the lemon halves
around them. Cover and leave to
marinate for 2 hours or overnight,
turning once or twice.

4 Turn the chicken pieces skin-side
up, scatter over the remaining
garlic cloves and place the lemon
halves cut-side down on top. Roast the
chicken in a preheated oven, 200°C,
400°F, Gas Mark 6, for 45 minutes or
until golden and tender. Stir in the
parsley and season to taste with salt
and pepper. Serve decorated with the
roasted lemon halves and garnished
with parsley sprigs.

1.75 kg (3½ lb) free-range chicken

4 ripe juicy lemons

8 garlic cloves

1 small red chilli, deseeded and
chopped

2 tablespoons orange flower honey

2 tablespoons chopped parsley

salt and pepper

flat leaf parsley sprigs, to garnish

Serves 4

Preparation time: 25 minutes,
plus marinating

Cooking time: 45 minutes

chicken with wild mushrooms

1 If using dried mushrooms, put them into a bowl and just cover with hot water. Leave to soak for 15 minutes.

2 Meanwhile, season the flour with salt and pepper and toss the chicken breasts in the seasoned flour, to cover all over. Heat the butter and oil in a frying pan, add the chicken breasts and cook for 4 minutes on each side or until golden. Remove the chicken and keep warm.

3 Add the shallots and garlic to the frying pan and sauté gently for 5 minutes. Add the wine and mix well to include any tasty brown bits from the pan. Add the mascarpone and the mushrooms to the pan; if using wild mushrooms, add the soaking liquid. Mix well to melt the mascarpone. If the mixture is very runny, turn up the heat to evaporate some of the liquid. If you are using fresh mushrooms, add a little extra liquid, but remember that mushrooms make their own liquid as they cook.

4 Return the chicken to the pan and simmer gently for 10 minutes, turning occasionally. Finally stir the chives into the pan and serve immediately, garnished with extra chives.

50 g (2 oz) dried wild mushrooms or 250 g (8 oz) fresh mushrooms, sliced

50 g (2 oz) plain flour

4 boneless, skinless chicken breasts

50 g (2 oz) butter

1 tablespoon olive oil

2 shallots, diced

2 garlic cloves, chopped

125 ml (4 fl oz) white wine

125 g (4 oz) mascarpone cheese

handful of chives, snipped, plus extra to garnish

salt and pepper

Serves 4

Preparation time: 15 minutes, plus soaking

Cooking time: about 30 minutes

chicken with ham & fennel

1 Season the chicken inside and out with salt and pepper. Mix together the ham, garlic and fennel stalks and leaves and stuff the chicken. Place in a deep casserole dish and spread the butter over the chicken.

2 Cover the casserole and cook in a preheated oven, 200°C (400°F), Gas Mark 6, for 1 hour. Remove the lid and continue cooking, basting frequently, for 20 minutes until tender. Remove the chicken with a slotted spoon, transfer to a warmed serving dish and keep hot.

3 Season the juices to taste with salt, pepper and lemon juice, and reheat. Serve the chicken, garnished with fennel leaves, accompanied by its juices.

1.75 kg (3½ lb) chicken

175 g (6 oz) cooked ham, cut into strips

2 garlic cloves, crushed

4 tablespoons chopped fennel stalks and leaves

40 g (1½ oz) butter, softened

lemon juice

salt and pepper

fennel leaves, to garnish

Serves 4
Preparation time: 10 minutes
Cooking time: 1¼–1½ hours

turkey breasts with parmesan, egg & spinach

1 Whisk one of the eggs with half of the Parmesan and season with salt and pepper. Heat a scant table-spoon of the oil in a 15 cm (6 inch) frying pan, pour in the egg and cook until golden, then turn over and cook on the other side. Make a second omelette in the same way.

2 Heat 1 tablespoon oil in another pan, and cook the spinach over a moderate heat until it softens. Season to taste with nutmeg, salt and pepper.

3 Place an omelette, half the spinach and 2 rashers of streaky bacon on each turkey fillet. Roll up towards the pointed end and secure with cocktail sticks, previously soaked in cold water, and string.

4 Melt the butter and 1 tablespoon oil in a flameproof casserole and brown the turkey. Pour on the wine, add the rosemary and season with salt and pepper. Cover and cook in a preheated oven, 180°C (350°F), Gas Mark 4, for 1–1¼ hours until the turkey is tender. Take the turkey fillets from the pan and remove the cocktail sticks and strings. Cut into thick slices and arrange on a dish. Pour over the cook-ing liquid and serve hot with fresh, steamed spinach.

2 eggs

50 g (2 oz) Parmesan cheese, grated

3–4 tablespoons olive oil

300 g (10 oz) spinach, chopped

pinch of nutmeg

4 rashers lean rindless streaky bacon

2 x 250–300 g (8–10 oz) turkey breast fillets

25 g (1 oz) butter

300 ml (10 fl oz) dry white wine

½ teaspoon chopped rosemary

salt and pepper

steamed spinach, to serve

Serves 4–6

Preparation time: 40–45 minutes

Cooking time: 1¼–1½ hours

1 Slightly flatten each poussin half. Heat the butter and oil in a large pan, add the rosemary and poussins, skin side down, and fry over a low heat for 8–10 minutes, or until golden. Turn over and cook the other sides for 8–10 minutes until tender and cooked through. Transfer the poussins to a warmed serving dish and keep hot.

2 Add the wine to the pan, stirring well to scrape up the sediment. Simmer, uncovered, until reduced by half. Add the cream and season to taste with salt and pepper, tilting the pan to mix, and continue cooking until a smooth sauce forms. Remove and discard the rosemary.

3 Pour the sauce over the poussins and garnish with rosemary sprigs. Serve with roast potatoes and mangetout.

2 poussins, halved lengthways

50 g (2 oz) butter

1 tablespoon olive oil

4 rosemary sprigs, plus extra to garnish

150 ml (¼ pint) red wine or port

150 ml (¼ pint) single cream

salt and pepper

roast potatoes and mangetout, to serve

Serves 2–4
Preparation time: 10 minutes
Cooking time: 20–25 minutes

poussins medici

■ Poussins, also known as spring chickens, weigh 375–625 g (12 oz–1¼ lb); a small one makes an adequate single serving. Double poussins, weighing about 1 kg (2 lb), have more flavour as they are slightly older birds.

quails with peas & gammon

1 Heat half the butter and the oil in a flameproof casserole and brown the quails all over. Remove from the pan and add half the diced gammon. Cook until lightly coloured, then return the quails to the pan with the wine and tomatoes. Season with salt and pepper and bring to the boil. Cover tightly and cook in a preheated oven,190°C (375°F), Gas Mark 5, for 20–25 minutes until the quails are tender.

2 Meanwhile, heat the remaining butter in a pan and cook the remaining gammon until it is golden brown. Add the peas and, if necessary, a little water. Season lightly with salt and pepper. Simmer gently until the peas are tender and all the liquid has evaporated. Keep hot.

3 Remove the cooked quails from the pan and remove any trussing strings. Place on a warmed serving dish and keep hot. Add the pea mixture to the pan and stir well over a gentle heat until the peas are coated with the sauce and are heated through. If necessary, add some chicken stock to the pan to give a coating consistency. Pile on the serving dish, garnish with chopped parsley and serve immediately with creamed potatoes.

50 g (2 oz) butter

1 tablespoon olive oil

4–8 quails, cleaned and trussed

125 g (4 oz) gammon steak, finely diced

150 ml (¼ pint) dry white wine

400 g (13 oz) can tomatoes, drained, deseeded and chopped

375 g (12 oz) shelled fresh or frozen peas

150 ml (¼ pint) chicken stock

salt and pepper

chopped flat leaf parsley, to garnish

creamed potatoes, to serve

Serves 4

Preparation time: 20–30 minutes

Cooking time: 40–50 minutes

creamy chicken livers with port

1 Heat the butter and oil in a heavy-based pan. Add the chicken livers and celery and fry for 3–4 minutes, until the livers are golden outside but still pink inside. Add the port and simmer for a few minutes, until slightly reduced.

2 Add the soured cream, tilting the pan to mix, and continue cooking gently until a smooth sauce forms. Season to taste with salt and pepper.

3 Garnish with celery leaves and serve with pasta tossed in garlic butter.

25 g (1 oz) butter

1 tablespoon olive oil

500 g (1 lb) chicken livers, trimmed and halved

3 celery sticks, sliced

4 tablespoons port

150 ml (¼ pint) soured cream

salt and pepper

pasta, tossed in garlic butter, to serve

celery leaves, to garnish

Serves 4
Preparation time: 5 minutes
Cooking time: 8–10 minutes

mushroom lasagne ●

fusilli with aubergines & tomato sauce ●

mozzarella & plum tomato lasagne with chilli ●

avocado & mushroom salad ●

country garden salad ●

fennel & pasta salad ●

herb sausage & garlic penne salad ●

warm penne, bean & asparagus salad ●

italian summer salad ●

adriatic salad ●

vegetables & salads

ortaggi e insalata

mushroom lasagne

1 Heat the oil in a frying pan, add the onion and fry over a moderate heat for 3 minutes, stirring frequently. Add the mushrooms and cook for 2 minutes. Stir in the pine nuts and ham, if using and sauté for 2 minutes. Add the cream cheese and milk and heat until the cheese melts. Season to taste with salt and pepper.

2 To make the white sauce, melt the butter in a saucepan and stir in the flour. Cook gently, stirring, for 1–2 minutes. Remove from the heat and slowly whisk in the milk. Return to the heat and bring slowly to the boil, whisking all the time until thick and smooth. Stir in three-quarters of the pecorino or Cheddar. Season to taste with salt and pepper.

3 To assemble the lasagne, drizzle 3 tablespoons of the sauce into a greased ovenproof dish. Arrange one-third of the lasagne sheets over the sauce, then add half of the mushroom mixture. Put another one-third of the lasagne sheets on top. Add the remaining mushroom mixture, the remaining lasagne and finally the cheese sauce. Sprinkle with the remaining cheeses and a generous pinch of pepper. Put the dish on a baking sheet and bake in a preheated oven, 190°C (375°F), Gas Mark 5, for 25–30 minutes or until golden brown. Leave to stand for 10 minutes then serve with a salad.

2 tablespoons olive oil

1 large onion, chopped

250 g (8 oz) button mushrooms

500 g (1 lb) mixed wild mushrooms, trimmed and sliced

2 tablespoons pine nuts

125 g (4 oz) ham, cut into slices (optional)

250 g (8 oz) garlic and herb cream cheese

4 tablespoons milk

250 g (8 oz) no-precook lasagne

125 g (4 oz) pecorino or Cheddar cheese, grated

25 g (1 oz) Parmesan cheese, grated

salt and pepper

salad, to serve

White Sauce:

40 g (1½ oz) butter

40 g (1½ oz) flour

600 ml (1 pint) milk

Serves 4

Preparation time: 25 minutes

Cooking time: 35 minutes

fusilli with aubergines & tomato sauce

1 Spread the diced aubergine on a wire cooling rack over a tray and sprinkle over 1–2 teaspoons salt. Leave for at least 30 minutes to drain. This will remove some of the liquid. Rinse thoroughly, drain well and dry on kitchen paper.

2 Meanwhile, make the tomato sauce. Heat the oil in a pan. Add the onion and garlic and fry over a fairly low heat, stirring frequently, for 5–7 minutes until the onion is soft but not coloured. Add the tomatoes and the sugar, season to taste with salt and pepper and simmer for about 30 minutes, until thickened.

3 Heat half the oil in a frying pan and cook some of the aubergine dice until they are golden brown. Repeat, adding more oil to the pan if necessary, until all the dice are cooked. Keep the cooked aubergine hot.

4 Cook the fusilli in lightly salted boiling water until just tender but still firm to the bite. Drain well and stir into the hot tomato sauce. Check and adjust the seasoning if necessary. Pour into a serving bowl and put the fried aubergine on top. Sprinkle the chopped basil or parsley over the top just before serving.

1 large aubergine, diced

125–150 ml (4–5 fl oz) olive oil

500 g (1 lb) dried fusilli

salt and pepper

1 tablespoon chopped basil or parsley, to garnish

Tomato Sauce:

1–2 tablespoons olive oil

1 onion, chopped

2 garlic cloves, crushed

400 g (13 oz) can chopped tomatoes

1 teaspoon sugar

Serves 4

Preparation time: 20 minutes, plus draining

Cooking time: 40–45 minutes

mozzarella & plum tomato lasagne with chilli

1 Line the base of a buttered 1.2 litre (2 pint) ovenproof dish with 2 sheets of lasagne, cutting them to fit if necessary. Slice 6 of the tomatoes and arrange half of the slices over the lasagne, packing them in well. Sprinkle with salt and add a few slices of mozzarella and goats' cheese and some oregano.

2 Lay 2 more lasagne sheets on top and cover with the remaining tomato slices, half of the remaining cheese slices and the remaining oregano. Top with the 2 remaining lasagne sheets.

3 Cut the 4 remaining tomatoes into wedges, and scatter over the pasta with the remaining cheese. Drizzle with the chilli-flavoured oil and cook in a preheated oven, 200°C (400°F), Gas Mark 6, for 20–30 minutes. Remove from the oven and leave to rest for 10 minutes before serving.

butter, for greasing

6 no-precook lasagne verde sheets

10 large plum tomatoes

125 g (4 oz) mozzarella cheese, sliced

125 g (4 oz) goats' cheese, sliced

1 small bunch of oregano, chopped

chilli-flavoured oil, for drizzling

salt

Serves 4
Preparation time: 10 minutes
Cooking time: 20–30 minutes

avocado & mushroom salad

1 Mix the dressing ingredients together and season to taste with salt and pepper. Put the mushrooms in a large bowl, pour over the dressing and toss well, until all the mushrooms are coated.

2 Arrange the frisée on a flat plate. Cut the lime or lemon in half. Squeeze the juice from one half and slice the other half. Slice the avocados and sprinkle with the lime or lemon juice to prevent browning. Arrange on top of the frisée.

3 Spoon the mushrooms on to the centre. Sprinkle the pine nuts over the salad and garnish with the lime or lemon slices. Serve immediately.

■ Pine nuts are used a lot in Italian cooking. They have a high oil content, so don't keep them too long or they will go rancid.

250 g (8 oz) button mushrooms, sliced

½ head of frisée lettuce

1 lime or lemon

2 large avocados

25 g (1 oz) pine nuts, toasted

Dressing:

6 tablespoons extra virgin olive oil

3–4 tablespoons lemon juice

1 teaspoon finely grated lemon rind

1 garlic clove, crushed

1 teaspoon crushed coriander seeds

1 teaspoon clear honey

salt and pepper

Serves 4

Preparation time: 10 minutes

250 g (8 oz) very small new potatoes

1 mint sprig

250 g (8 oz) carrots, quartered lengthways

250 g (8 oz) peas

125 g (4 oz) small green beans

1 thin leek, sliced

salt and pepper

Dressing:

4 tablespoons extra virgin olive oil

2 tablespoons lemon juice

1 teaspoon mustard

½ teaspoon clear honey

1 garlic clove, crushed

2 tablespoons chopped mint

1 Cook the potatoes in salted boiling water with the sprig of mint for 10–12 minutes until tender. Drain and refresh under cold running water. Drain again thoroughly.

2 Meanwhile, cook the carrots in salted boiling water for 7–10 minutes, add the peas and beans to the pan and cook for a further 3 minutes. Drain the vegetables and refresh under cold running water. Drain again thoroughly.

3 Put the cooked vegetables in a large bowl and allow to cool. Add the leek. Mix the dressing ingredients together and season to taste with salt and pepper. Spoon over the vegetables and mix well. Pile the salad into a serving bowl and serve immediately.

Serves 4

Preparation time: 10 minutes

Cooking time: 15 minutes

country garden salad

fennel & pasta salad

1 Cook the pasta in lightly salted boiling water for 8–10 minutes, until tender but still firm to the bite. Drain and refresh under cold running water. Drain again thoroughly and place in a large bowl.

2 Toss the fennel and apples in the lemon juice, then add to the pasta with the spring onions and tomatoes. Mix together gently.

3 Mix the dressing ingredients together and pour over the salad. Transfer to a serving bowl. Sprinkle with the sesame seeds and cashew nuts and garnish with fennel leaves. Serve immediately.

■ Fennel, sometimes called Florence fennel, has a strong liquorice flavour. People either love it or hate it – but its worth trying once.

500 g (1 lb) dried conchiglie

3 large fennel bulbs, thinly sliced

2–3 red apples, cored and sliced

4 tablespoons lemon juice

4 spring onions, chopped

4 tomatoes, skinned, deseeded and chopped (see page 35)

2 tablespoons sesame seeds, toasted

50 g (2 oz) salted cashew nuts

fennel leaves, to garnish

Dressing:

6 tablespoons olive oil

3 tablespoons lemon juice

1 teaspoon French mustard

1 teaspoon clear honey

Serves 4–6
Preparation time: 15 minutes
Cooking time: 8–10 minutes

herb sausage & garlic penne salad

1 Grill the sausages until cooked through and crisp on the outside. Remove from the heat and leave to cool for 10 minutes.

2 Meanwhile, cook the pasta in lightly salted boiling water for 8–10 minutes, until tender but still firm to the bite.

3 Drain the pasta, rinse under cold water in a colander and drain again. Transfer to a large salad bowl. Mix the garlic, shallot, gherkins, olive oil and parsley in a bowl. Add to the pasta, season to taste with salt and pepper and toss well to combine.

4 Cut the sausages into large chunks and stir them into the salad, then garnish with chopped parsley. Serve immediately or chill until required.

250 g (8 oz) herb pork sausages

300 g (10 oz) dried penne

1–2 garlic cloves, crushed

1 shallot, finely chopped

2 gherkins, finely chopped

3 tablespoons olive oil

1 tablespoon chopped parsley, plus extra to garnish

salt and pepper

Serves 4

Preparation time: 10 minutes

Cooking time: 25 minutes

warm penne, bean & asparagus salad

1 Cook the penne in lightly salted boiling water until tender but still firm to the bite.

2 Meanwhile, steam the asparagus for 10–12 minutes. Alternatively, place on a baking sheet, brush with olive oil and place under a preheated hot grill for 8 minutes, turning as the pieces brown.

3 Cook the broad beans or peas in lightly salted boiling water for 2 minutes, or until tender. Drain the pasta and pour the crème fraîche into the empty pasta pan over the heat. Add the beans or peas, asparagus and Parmesan. Heat gently and season to taste with salt and pepper. Return the pasta to the pan, add the mint and toss well. Serve garnished with Parmesan and mint.

300 g (10 oz) penne

500 g (1 lb) asparagus, trimmed and cut into 5 cm (2 inch) lengths

2 tablespoons olive oil

250 g (8 oz) broad beans or peas

75 ml (3 fl oz) crème fraîche

50 g (2 oz) Parmesan cheese, grated, plus extra to garnish

4 tablespoons chopped mint, plus extra to garnish

salt and pepper

Serves 4

Preparation time: 10 minutes

Cooking time: 20 minutes

■ Make this dish with any variety of small pasta shapes that you happen to have in your storecupboard.

4 carrots, grated

1 tablespoon chopped parsley

2 small fennel bulbs, sliced

juice of ½ lemon

1 tablespoon chopped thyme

2 large tomatoes

125 g (4 oz) mozzarella cheese

175 g (6 oz) spinach

1 head radicchio

50 g (2 oz) salted cashew nuts

Dressing:

6 tablespoons olive oil

3 tablespoons lemon juice

1 teaspoon each grated lemon rind, French mustard and clear honey

1–2 garlic cloves, crushed

3 tablespoons chopped basil

salt and pepper

Serves 4
Preparation time: 10 minutes
Cooking time: 20–30 minutes

1 Mix together the carrots and parsley and set aside. Combine the fennel, lemon juice and thyme.

2 Arrange the carrots on one quarter of a large platter and the fennel on the next quarter. Slice the tomatoes and mozzarella and arrange alternately in the third quarter.

3 Tear the spinach and radicchio leaves into pieces and arrange on the remaining quarter of the platter. Sprinkle with the nuts.

4 Mix together all the dressing ingredients and season to taste with salt and pepper. Spoon over the salad and serve immediately.

italian summer salad

adriatic salad

1 Soak the mussels in a bowl of cold water. Scrub them well to remove any barnacles and then remove the beards. Discard any that do not close when sharply tapped with a knife.

2 Put the mussels, scallops and haddock in a shallow pan and pour over the vermouth and stock. Add the bouquet garni and season with salt and pepper. Bring to the boil and cook, shaking the pan frequently, for 4 minutes, until the mussel shells have opened and the haddock is cooked through.

3 Carefully remove the fish and seafood from the stock with a slotted spoon, discarding any mussels that have not opened. Remove the shells. Place all the cooked fish in a bowl and allow to cool, then add the crab meat and prawns, mix well.

4 To make the dressing, mix all the ingredients and season to taste with salt and pepper. Add to the fish mixture and mix gently. To serve, arrange the lettuce on individual dishes, then spoon the prepared seafood on top. Serve lightly chilled.

20 live mussels

4 scallops, shelled

250 g (8 oz) smoked haddock

150 ml (¼ pint) dry vermouth

150 ml (¼ pint) fish stock

1 bouquet garni

175 g (6 oz) fresh or canned crab meat, flaked

125 g (4 oz) cooked peeled prawns

salt and pepper

2 small lettuces, to serve

Dressing:

50 ml (2 fl oz) mayonnaise

50 g (2 oz) Greek yogurt

2 hard-boiled eggs, chopped

1 tablespoon capers

½ cucumber, diced

Serves 4–6
Preparation time: 15 minutes, plus chilling
Cooking time: 5 minutes

pizzas, calzoni & breads

pizze, calzoni & pane

artichoke & mushroom pizza

1 To make pizza dough sift the flour, yeast and salt into a bowl. Make a well in the centre and add the oil. Gradually pour in the water. Stir vigorously, drawing in the flour a little at a time, to form a soft dough. Knead for at least 10 minutes until the dough feels smooth and springy. Place in an oiled bowl, turn once so the surface is coated, then cover the bowl with a cloth and leave to rise in a warm place for 1–2 hours until doubled in size. Knock back the dough and turn it out on to a floured surface. Knead again for 2–3 minutes.

2 Roll out the dough to a 30 cm (12 inch) circle, making the edge thicker than the rest, and place on a greased baking sheet.

3 Pour the oil from the artichokes into a bowl, stir in lemon juice to taste and use to brush over the pizza base. Slice the artichokes in half.

4 Heat the olive oil in a frying pan, add the oyster mushrooms and fry for 5–6 minutes. Toss the mushrooms with the artichokes and spread evenly over the pizza base. Scatter over the grated mozzarella. Bake in a preheated oven, 240°C (475°F), Gas Mark 9, for about 15 minutes, garnish with the chopped oregano and serve immediately.

400 g (13 oz) can artichokes in oil, drained and oil reserved

1 tablespoon lemon juice, or to taste

olive oil, for frying

125 g (4 oz) oyster mushrooms, sliced

125 g (4 oz) mozzarella cheese, grated

chopped oregano, to garnish

Pizza Dough:

250 g (8 oz) unbleached strong plain flour

1 teaspoon easy-blend dried yeast

1 teaspoon salt

1 tablespoon olive oil

125–150 ml (4–5 fl oz) tepid water

Serves 4
Preparation time: 10 minutes, plus making the dough
Cooking time: about 20 minutes

mixed tomato & basil pizza

1 Roll out the dough on a lightly floured surface to a 30 cm (12 inch) circle, making the edge thicker than the rest. Place on a greased baking sheet.

2 Brush the pizza base with 1 table-spoon of the oil. Arrange the large tomatoes and torn basil leaves over the pizza, then place the cherry tomatoes and sun-dried tomatoes over the top.

3 Heat the remaining oil in a small pan, add the garlic and fry gently until it starts to colour. Drizzle the garlic and its cooking oil over the tomatoes. Using a vegetable peeler, shave the Parmesan over the pizza.

4 Bake the pizza in a preheated oven, 200°C (400°F), Gas Mark 6, for 20 minutes. Serve immediately.

1 quantity Pizza Dough (see page 80)

3 tablespoons olive oil or oil from the sun-dried tomatoes

500 g (1 lb) large tomatoes, sliced

handful of torn basil leaves

125 g (4 oz) yellow cherry tomatoes, halved

50 g (2 oz) sun-dried tomatoes in oil, drained and sliced

3 garlic cloves, sliced

50 g (2 oz) Parmesan cheese

salt and pepper

Serves 4

Preparation time: 20 minutes, plus making the dough

Cooking time: about 20 minutes

■ The pizza dough should be knocked back to expel the air (slap it down on a floured sur-face two or three times) and then knead again for several minutes, until it is elastic.

mozzarella
& red pesto pizza

1 Make the pizza dough according to the instructions on page 80, adding the chopped rosemary at the same time as the olive oil.

2 To make the red pesto, place the garlic, pine nuts, sun-dried tomatoes and basil in a food processor or blender and process until fairly smooth. Alternatively, grind in a mortar with a pestle. Gradually beat in the olive oil, then stir in the Parmesan. Taste and season with salt and pepper, if necessary.

3 Roll the dough out to a 30 cm (12 inch) circle and place on a greased baking sheet. Spread the red pesto over the pizza base and sprinkle with the diced mozzarella. Arrange the cherry tomatoes and olives on the top and bake in a preheated oven, 220°C (425°F), Gas Mark 7, for 15–20 minutes. Serve hot.

■ Now made throughout Italy and many other countries, mozzarella cheese originated in Latium and Campania. It was originally made from buffalo milk and this, known as *mozzarella di bufala*, is still available. However, the majority is now made from cows' milk and has a slightly blander flavour.

Fresh Rosemary Dough:

1 quantity Pizza Dough (see page 80)

1 tablespoon rosemary leaves, finely chopped

Red Pesto:

1 garlic clove, crushed

25 g (1 oz) pine nuts

50 g (2 oz) sun-dried tomatoes in oil, drained and sliced

25 g (1 oz) basil leaves

75 ml (3 fl oz) extra virgin olive oil

2 tablespoons grated Parmesan cheese

Topping:

125 g (4 oz) mozzarella cheese, diced

125 g (4 oz) cherry tomatoes, halved

50 g (2 oz) black olives, pitted

salt and pepper

Serves 4–6

Preparation time: 30 minutes, plus making the dough

Cooking time: 15–20 minutes

asparagus & tomato pan pizza

1 Mix together the tomato purée, garlic, basil and oregano.

2 Lightly grease a very large heavy-based frying pan. Roll out the dough on a floured board to the size of the pan. Place in the pan and bring a little dough up the sides.

3 Grate a quarter of the mozzarella and sprinkle it over the pizza base. Spoon the tomato purée mixture on top. Dice the remaining mozzarella. Arrange the tomatoes and asparagus over the pizza and sprinkle with the mozzarella and Parmesan.

4 Cook over a medium heat for 15–20 minutes, then place under a preheated grill for 1–2 minutes, until golden. Serve immediately.

65 g (2½ oz) tomato purée

1 garlic clove, crushed

½ teaspoon dried basil

½ teaspoon dried oregano

1 quantity Pizza Dough (see page 80)

125 g (4 oz) mozzarella cheese

250 g (8 oz) tomatoes, skinned and sliced

250 g (8 oz) cooked or canned asparagus

1 tablespoon grated Parmesan cheese

Serves 4

Preparation time: 30 minutes, plus making the dough

Cooking time: about 20 minutes

1 Place the aubergine in a colander, sprinkle with salt and leave for 30 minutes to drain. Rinse under cold running water, drain and pat dry with kitchen paper.

2 Heat the oil in a large saucepan, add the onion and fry until softened. Stir in the garlic and red pepper and fry for 5 minutes. Add the aubergine, chopped tomatoes and tomato purée and season to taste with salt and pepper. Bring the mixture to the boil, then lower the heat, cover and simmer for about 20 minutes. Add the courgettes and basil leaves and cook for 5 minutes. Remove the pan from the heat.

3 Divide the pizza dough in half. Roll out each piece on a lightly floured surface to a 20 cm (8 inch) round, making the edges slightly thicker. Place on greased baking sheets.

4 Place half of the ratatouille on one half of each round, brush the edges of the dough with water and fold the rounds in half. Press well to seal, and pinch the edges together. Brush the calzoni with a little olive oil and sprinkle over the Parmesan. Bake in a preheated oven, 200°C (400°F), Gas Mark 6, for 20–25 minutes until risen and golden. Serve hot.

ratatouille calzoni

1 aubergine, cubed

2 tablespoons olive oil

1 onion, chopped

2 garlic cloves, crushed

1 red pepper, cored, deseeded and chopped

400 g (13 oz) can chopped tomatoes

1 tablespoon tomato purée

2 courgettes, sliced

1 tablespoon torn basil leaves

1 quantity Pizza Dough (see page 80)

2 tablespoons freshly grated Parmesan cheese

salt and pepper

Makes 2 calzoni

Preparation time: 20 minutes, plus draining and making the dough

Cooking time: about 1 hour

focaccia with sun-dried tomatoes

1 Blend the yeast with half of the warm water, 125 g (4 oz) of the flour and the sugar until evenly combined and leave in a warm place for about 10 minutes until frothy.

2 Sift the remaining flour into a large bowl with the salt and semolina and gradually work in the yeast liquid and the oil from the sun-dried tomatoes, stirring the dry ingredients into the liquid to make a smooth but not wet dough. Add a little more water if necessary. Turn on to a floured surface and knead until smooth and elastic. Transfer to an oiled bowl, turn once to coat the dough. Cover and leave to rise for about 45 minutes until doubled in size.

3 Knock back the dough on a floured surface by kneading gently. Work in the sun-dried tomatoes. Roll into a large flat oval and transfer to a greased baking sheet. Brush with olive oil and sprinkle with sea salt. Using the end of a wooden spoon, make deep indentations over the surface of the dough. Bake in a preheated oven, 220°C (425°F), Gas Mark 7, for 30–35 minutes until risen and golden. Serve warm.

15 g (½ oz) fresh yeast

300 ml (½ pint) warm water

300 g (10 oz) strong white flour

pinch of sugar

1 teaspoon salt

175 g (6 oz) fine semolina

2 tablespoons oil from the sun-dried tomatoes in oil

30 g (1¼ oz) sun-dried tomatoes in oil, finely chopped

olive oil, for brushing

coarse sea salt

Makes 1 loaf

Preparation time: 15 minutes, plus rising

Cooking time: 30–35 minutes

gorgonzola focaccia

1 Blend the yeast with half of the warm water, 125 g (4 oz) of the flour and the sugar until combined. Leave in a warm place for about 10 minutes until frothy.

2 Put the remaining flour into a large bowl, add the semolina and salt and gradually work in the frothy yeast, 2 tablespoons olive oil and enough of the remaining water to make a stiff dough. Knead for 10 minutes until smooth and elastic. Transfer to an oiled bowl, turning once to coat the dough. Cover and leave to rise for about 45 minutes until doubled in size.

3 Tip the dough on to a lightly floured surface and knead for 2–3 minutes. Work in the Gorgonzola, then shape into a large flat oval. Transfer to a greased baking sheet, brush with oil and sprinkle with coarse salt. With the end of a wooden spoon make deep indentations over the surface of the dough. Bake in a preheated oven, 220°C (425°F), Gas Mark 7, for 30–35 minutes until risen. Serve slightly warm.

15 g (½ oz) fresh yeast

300 ml (½ pint) warm water

300 g (10 oz) strong white flour

175 g (6 oz) fine semolina

1 teaspoon salt

pinch of sugar

175 g (6 oz) Gorgonzola cheese, chopped

3–5 tablespoons virgin olive oil, plus extra for brushing

coarse sea salt

Makes 1 loaf

Preparation time: 30 minutes, plus rising

Cooking time: 30–35 minutes

chocolate semi-freddo •

coffee hazelnut ice •

chocolate & hazelnut parfait •

vanilla pears in vin santo •

chocolate pistachio biscotti •

crostata di ricotta •

desserts & baking

dolce specialità al forno

chocolate semi-freddo

1 Beat the mascarpone in a bowl with the brandy, espresso coffee and icing sugar. Reserve 1 tablespoon of the grated chocolate and stir the remainder, together with the single cream, into the mixture.

2 Whip the double cream until just peaking and fold into the mascarpone mixture, using a large metal spoon.

3 Turn the chocolate mixture into a freezer container and freeze for 2–3 hours.

4 To serve, scoop the semi-freddo into serving glasses or coffee cups. Drizzle with a little coffee liqueur, if liked. Decorate with lightly whipped cream and serve sprinkled with the reserved grated chocolate.

250 g (8 oz) mascarpone cheese

2 tablespoons brandy

2 tablespoons fine ground espresso coffee

25 g (1 oz) icing sugar

75 g (3 oz) bitter or plain chocolate, grated

5 tablespoons single cream

300 ml (½ pint) double cream

To Decorate:

coffee liqueur (optional)

lightly whipped cream

Serves 5–6

Preparation time: 10 minutes, plus freezing

1 Reserve a few nuts for decoration, then grind the remainder coarsely. Place the milk in a saucepan and bring almost to the boil. Cream together the egg yolks and sugar until pale, then gradually stir in the hot milk. Stir in the ground nuts.

2 Pour into a clean saucepan and heat gently, stirring constantly, until the mixture is thick enough to coat the back of the spoon. Do not allow it to boil. Stir in the coffee, mixing well to blend. Cover and leave until cold, stirring occasionally.

3 Fold the cream into the coffee custard. Turn into individual containers, cover and freeze until firm. Transfer to the refrigerator 1 hour before serving to soften. Decorate with the reserved nuts and mint sprigs and serve with dessert biscuits.

100 g (3½ oz) hazelnuts, toasted and skinned

300 ml (½ pint) milk

4 egg yolks

75 g (3 oz) caster sugar

1 tablespoon instant coffee granules

175 ml (6 fl oz) whipping cream, whipped

mint sprigs, to decorate

dessert biscuits, to serve

Serves 4–5

Preparation time: 15 minutes, plus cooling and freezing

Cooking time: 8–10 minutes

coffee hazelnut ice

chocolate & hazelnut parfait

125 g (4 oz) blanched hazelnuts

125 g (4 oz) very dark chocolate, broken into pieces

600 ml (1 pint) double cream

2 eggs, separated

175 g (6 oz) icing sugar

dessert biscuits, to serve

To Decorate:

chocolate curls

cocoa powder

Serves 4

Preparation time: 10 minutes, plus freezing

1 Spread the hazelnuts on a baking sheet and toast in a preheated oven, 160°C (325°F), Gas Mark 3, for 5–10 minutes until golden. Leave them to cool completely then grind very finely.

2 Place the chocolate in a heat-proof bowl over a pan of hot water and leave to melt. Whisk the cream until it holds its shape, then fold in the nuts. Whisk the egg yolks in a large bowl with 2 tablespoons of the sugar until they are pale and creamy. Whisk the egg whites in another bowl until they form soft peaks, then add the remaining sugar, spoonful by spoonful, whisking between each addition until the mixture is very thick.

3 Stir the chocolate into the egg yolk mixture. Fold in the cream, then the meringue mixture. Turn the mixture into individual ice cream moulds or a freezer container and freeze for 12 hours until firm.

4 To serve, remove the parfait from the freezer and transfer it to the refrigerator to soften for 10 minutes. Decorate with chocolate curls and dust with cocoa powder. Serve with dessert biscuits.

vanilla pears in vin santo

1 Heat the vin santo or sherry in a large saucepan with the vanilla pod. Peel the pears carefully, but leave their stalks intact.

2 Stand the pears in the saucepan, they should just fit cosily, and spoon over a little wine to prevent them discolouring. Cover the pan tightly so that no liquid is lost and poach the pears gently for about 25 minutes, turning them in the liquid occasionally, until they are tender. Leave to cool in the liquid.

3 Remove the vanilla pod from the pan, scrape out the seeds and reserve them. Lift the pears from the wine and place them on a serving dish.

4 Add the reserved vanilla seeds to the liquid in the saucepan and boil until it has reduced to 300 ml (½ pint). Mix the arrowroot with a little cold water, then pour into the pan and whisk over the heat until the sauce has thickened. Stir in the vanilla essence. Leave the sauce to cool then pour it over the pears. Sprinkle the pears with the chopped toasted hazelnuts to decorate.

600 ml (1 pint) vin santo or sherry

1 vanilla pod, split open

6 firm but ripe dessert pears

2 teaspoons arrowroot

1 teaspoon vanilla essence

chopped toasted hazelnuts, to decorate

Serves 6

Preparation time: 10 minutes, plus standing and cooling

Cooking time: about 30 minutes

chocolate pistachio biscotti

1 Lightly grease a baking sheet. Put the chocolate in a heatproof bowl with the butter and heat very gently over a pan of simmering water until the chocolate has melted. Remove from the heat and cool slightly.

2 Sift the flour and baking powder into a bowl. Add the sugar, polenta, lemon rind, brandy, egg and pistachio nuts. Add the chocolate and mix to make a soft dough. Divide the mixture in half. Using lightly floured hands, shape each half into a sausage, about 28 cm (11 inches) long.

3 Transfer the dough to the prepared baking sheet and flatten the rolls until they are about 1.5 cm (¾ inch) thick. Bake in a preheated oven, 160°C (325°F), Gas Mark 3, for 20 minutes, until risen and firm.

4 Leave to cool, then cut each piece diagonally into thin biscuits. Return the biscuits to the baking sheet, spacing them slightly apart, and bake for a further 10 minutes, or until crisp. Transfer to a wire rack to cool. Dust with icing sugar and store in an airtight tin for up to 1 week.

■ Polenta is a fine, golden cornmeal that is widely used in both savoury and sweet dishes.

175 g (6 oz) plain chocolate, broken into pieces

25 g (1 oz) lightly salted butter

200 g (7 oz) self-raising flour

1½ teaspoons baking powder

75 g (3 oz) caster sugar

50 g (2 oz) polenta

finely grated rind of 1 lemon

2 teaspoons brandy

1 egg, lightly beaten

75 g (3 oz) pistachio nuts

icing sugar, for dusting

Makes about 24

Preparation time: 20 minutes, plus cooling

Cooking time: 40 minutes

crostata di ricotta

1 Sift the flour and salt into a mixing bowl and rub in the butter with the fingertips until the mixture resembles fine breadcrumbs. Mix in the egg yolk and just enough iced water to form a soft dough. Knead lightly and leave to chill in the refrigerator for 30 minutes. Roll out the pastry and use to line a 20 cm (8 inch) flan ring. Reserve the pastry trimmings.

2 To make the filling, rub the ricotta cheese through a sieve into a bowl and then beat in the sugar and the eggs. Add the almonds, mixed peel, lemon rind, orange rind and juice and vanilla essence, beating well. Pour the filling into the prepared pastry case and smooth the surface.

3 Roll out the pastry trimmings and cut them into strips 1 cm (½ inch) wide. Arrange them in a lattice pattern over the top of the flan. Bake in a preheated oven, 180°C (350°F), Gas Mark 4, for 45–50 minutes, or until set and golden. Cool and serve cold, dusted with icing sugar.

◾ Ricotta is a creamy whey cheese, with a smooth texture and a slightly sweet flavour. It is used in a wide variety of dishes.

250 g (8 oz) plain flour

pinch of salt

125 g (4 oz) butter

1 egg yolk

2–3 tablespoons iced water

icing sugar, for dusting

Filling:

375 g (12 oz) ricotta cheese

75 g (3 oz) caster sugar

3 eggs, well beaten

50 g (2 oz) blanched almonds, finely chopped

75 g (3 oz) chopped mixed peel

finely grated rind of ½ lemon

juice and finely grated rind of ½ orange

¼ teaspoon vanilla essence

Serves 6–8

Preparation time: 20 minutes, plus chilling

Cooking time: 45–50 minutes

index